INTELLIGENT ANIMALS YOU NEED TO MEET

Animal Books Age 8
Children's Animal Books

BABY PROFESSOR

EDUCATION KIDS

Speedy Publishing LLC

40 E. Main St. #1156

Newark, DE 19711

www.speedypublishing.com

Copyright 2017

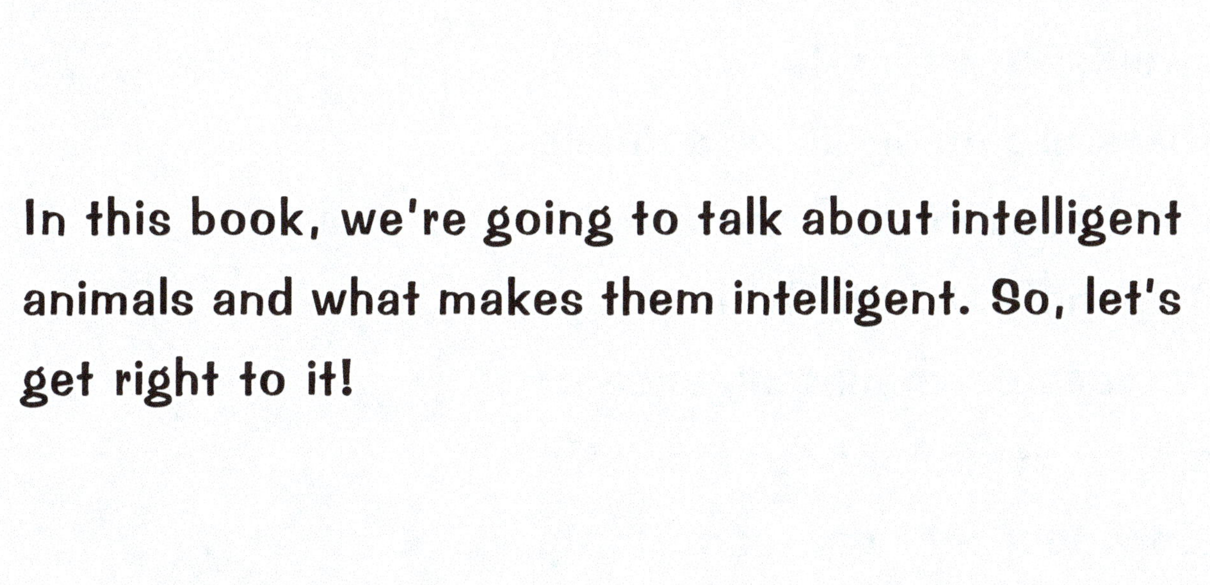

In this book, we're going to talk about intelligent animals and what makes them intelligent. So, let's get right to it!

Humans are not the only intelligent animals on Earth. There are many other animals that have forms of intelligence. Scientists are still finding ways to measure the intelligence of different animal species. No individual test can accurately measure their intelligence.

Dog

Rat

The reason is that some animals are excellent in learning by one method, but not so good at others. For example, rats have an excellent sense of smell. They can learn quickly if they are allowed to use smelling to figure something out. However, they don't do well at all on tests where they have to use their sense of sight.

Here are some of the most intelligent animals on Earth and the reasons why scientists think they're intelligent.

CHIMPANZEES

If you compare the DNA of a chimpanzee with the DNA of a human being, the match would be about 99%. Chimpanzees live in communities and are social creatures, which is one of the signs of intelligence. If their environment changes, they can respond quickly to the changes, which is another sign of intelligence. Even though they haven't created a language that's like a human language, humans have taught them how to use sign language.

Chimpanzee

Another common measure of intelligence is the ability to use tools. Chimps use stones to crack nuts open and they also use leaves to collect water to drink.

Chimpanzees share other characteristics with humans too. They can walk on two legs when they want to. They are omnivores, which means they eat plants as well as animals. They reach puberty about the same time as humans do too. The females reach reproductive age at about 13-years-old and the males at about 16-years-old.

Chimpanzee eating apple

Bottlenose Dolphin

BOTTLENOSE DOLPHINS

Just like human beings have names to identify themselves, bottlenose dolphins each have a unique whistle that is different from any other dolphin. A mother dolphin can tell if her baby is calling her, because the baby's whistle is different than all the others. If dolphins want to communicate with another dolphin, they mimic that dolphin's whistle to make contact. It's their way of communicating by name.

Bottlenose dolphins and other species of dolphins are social animals. They care about the members of their group. If a dolphin is ill, the others in the group try to help by surrounding the ill dolphin so it can stay at the water's surface to breathe.

There are many reports of dolphins that have helped human swimmers by circling in the water around them to protect them from sharks. There are even reports of pods of dolphins swimming aggressively toward sharks to get them away from humans.

Even more surprising is that bottlenose dolphins have teamed up with fishermen to help them catch fish. The dolphins swim in groups and force the schools of fish to come close to the shore. Then they splash around with head or tail slaps to signal that it's time for the fishermen to throw out their nets. The fishermen take in the fish, and the dolphins hunt the fish that aren't captured in the nets.

Bottlenose Dolphins

Scientists have also shown that dolphins recognize themselves in mirrors, which is another test of intelligence.

ELEPHANTS

Elephants are big and they have big brains too. In fact, they have the largest brains of all land animals. The cortex of the brain is the part of the brain responsible for thought as well as action. Studies show that the cortex of an elephant's brain has just as many neurons as a human being's brain. Not only can elephants learn, they also display that they are self-aware. Just like dolphins, they know themselves when they look in a mirror.

Elephant

Herd of Elephants

Like other intelligent animals, elephants are very social. They can form friendships that last their entire lives. They have compassion for each other and help each other. When an elephant that belongs to a group dies, the other elephants are sad and grieve in the place where their friend died.

Elephants communicate with each other in many different ways. They use their trunks as well as their ears and tails to send signals to one another. Using their trunks, they trumpet loudly over long distances to warn each other. They also make sounds, which humans can't hear, to communicate over long distances. Because they are so big, when their feet hit the ground, the vibrations travel over far distances. Elephants use these vibrations as another way to communicate with each other.

African Grey Parrot

AFRICAN GREY PARROTS

African Grey parrots have sometimes been called the "Einsteins" of the world of birds. They can reason, and understand that for every cause there is an effect. They can be taught to count and to learn as many as 1,000 human words. Once they learn human vocabulary, they can use the words to communicate with their owners.

Scientists believe that they have the mental capabilities of a human child at around age 5. Because African Grey parrots are so intelligent, they can also be needy like toddlers can be. They want to be amused with toys and be social with their owners. If they don't get enough attention, they can throw a tantrum just like a naughty child.

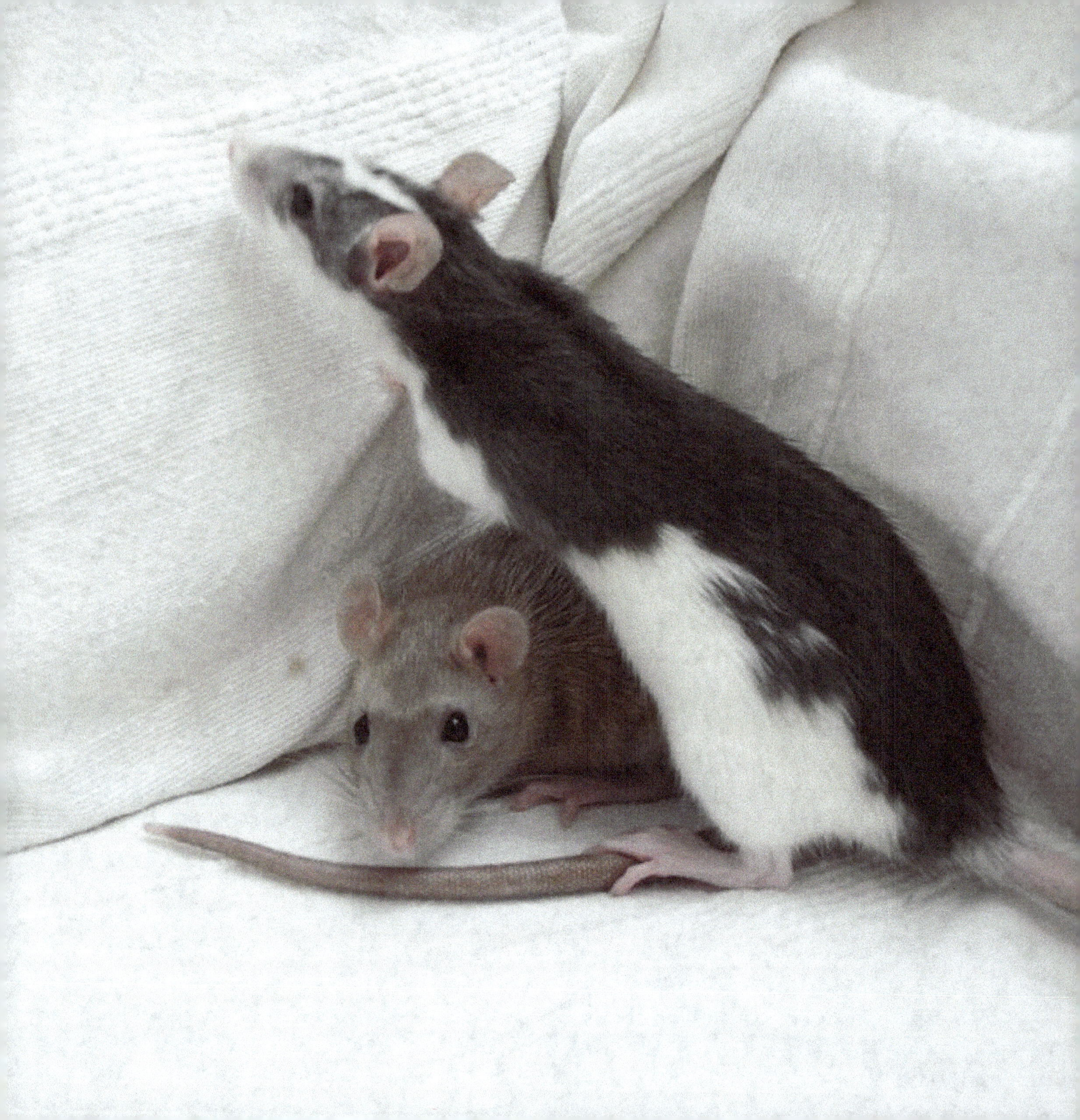

RATS

When rats go to sleep at night, they dream and a lot of their dreaming has to do with problems they need to solve. When you know that you know the answer to something but can't recall it at the moment you're asked, that's an example of metacognition.

It means you are thinking about your own thinking process. Several years ago, scientists found out that rats have metacognition too. They can make decisions and solve problems based on what they know or don't know.

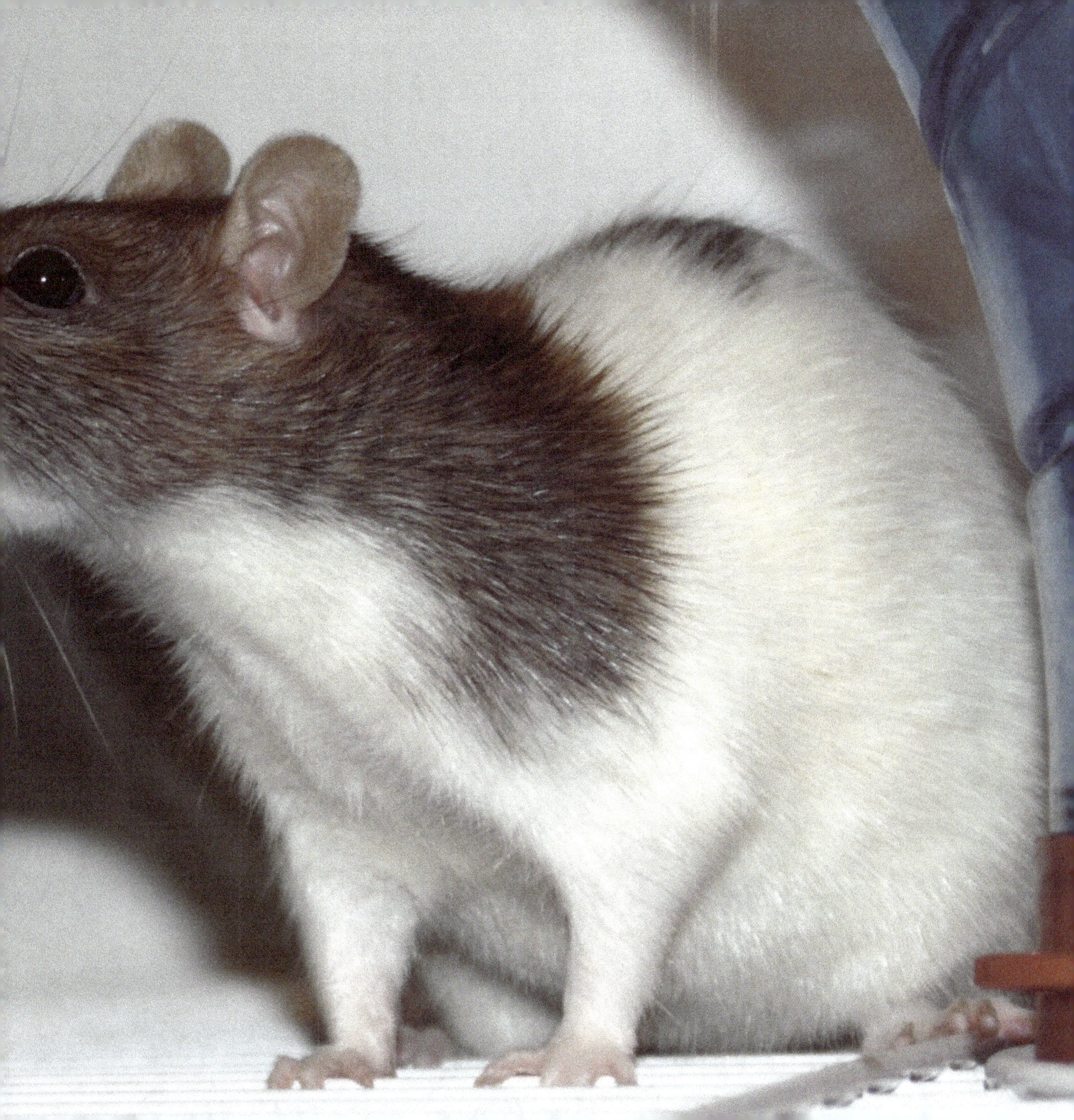

Rat

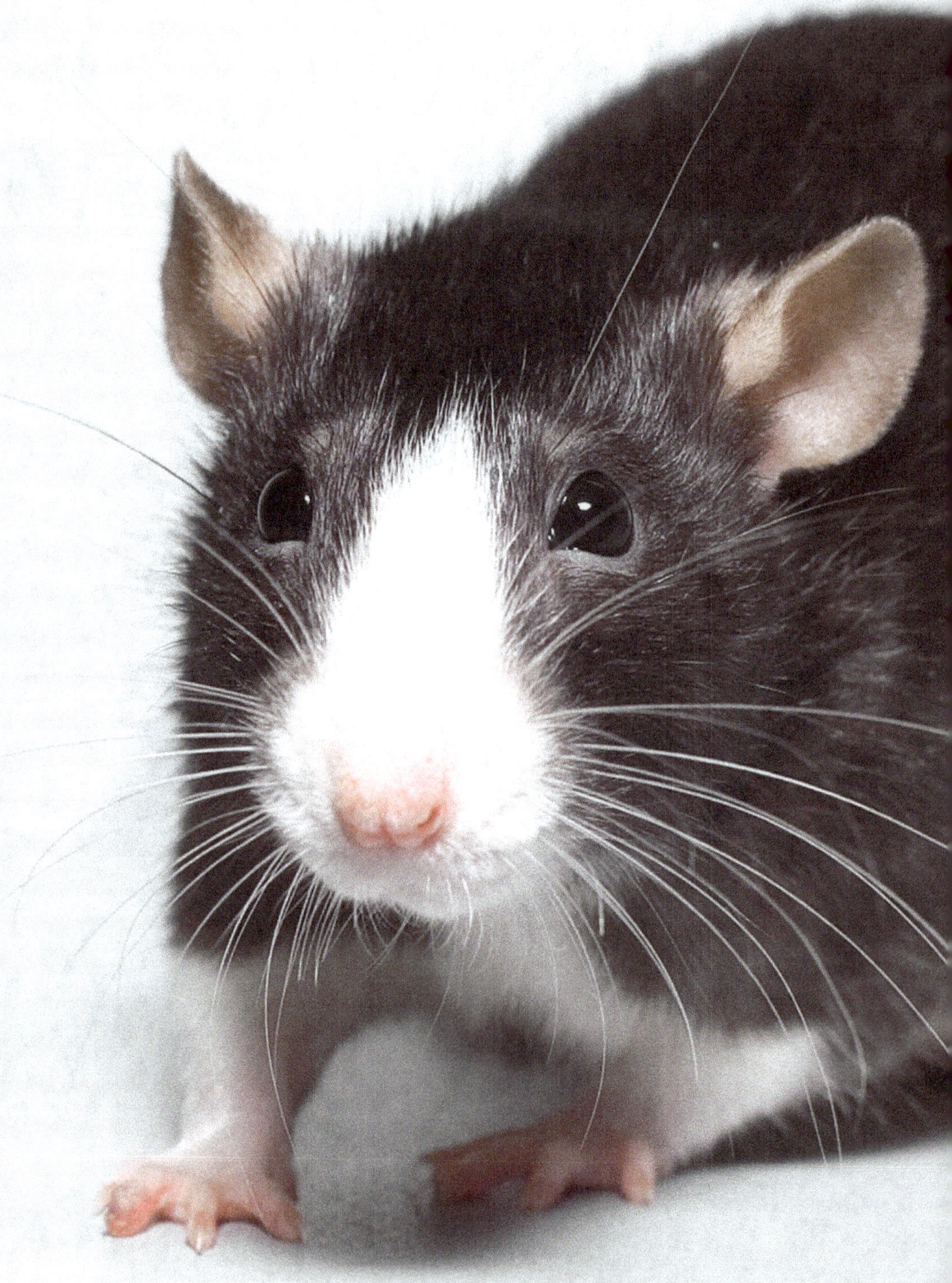

Rats have self-awareness and they're social too. In fact, pet rats become very attached to their owners. A pet rat can learn its name and will come when its owner calls it. Pet rats show their owners that they want to be let out of their cages so they can play with humans.

CROWS

Scientists believe that crows have an intelligence level that's similar to primates. Their brains are about the size of a human thumb, which doesn't seem that large, but it is compared to their body size. They can solve complicated problems.

Crows can be trained and they remember different people's faces. Scientists have shown that if someone is threatening or, on the other hand, if someone is kind, a crow will remember that person's face.

In Seattle, Washington there is an amazing case of an 8-year-old girl who has formed a special friendship with the crows in her backyard. She has feeders for them and to say "thank you" the crows bring her special trinkets. She believes that they have been able to figure out the items she likes and she's catalogued more than 70 gifts they've brought to her.

DOGS

Dogs have lived with people for thousands of years. Human beings judge a dog's intelligence by how well it can perform once it is asked to do something. However, some dogs that aren't obedient are still smart. Perhaps they just don't want to do what their owners want them to do, like take a bath!

Different breeds have varying levels of intelligence. In many ways, dogs are more like human beings than chimpanzees because they've lived with people for so long. Scientists believe that dogs have the learning ability of two-year old children.

Pigeon

PIGEONS

It's surprising that pigeons are so intelligent. Given math problems on a computer screen that involved ranking different patterns of numbers, pigeons scored the same as rhesus monkeys!

Pigeons have been trained to carry messages since ancient times. Scientists have also found that pigeons recognize the faces of different human beings. They also recognize themselves, if they see an image of themselves in a mirror. In 1995, a famous scientific experiment showed that pigeons that were trained could tell which paintings were painted by Monet and which paintings were painted by Picasso.

Carrier Pigeon

PIGS

Some scientists believe that pigs are the smartest domestic animals, even when compared with dogs and cats. They're also the cleanest, which seems odd because we always think of pigs in mud. Pigs roll in mud because they need the mud to cool off since they can't sweat like other animals. Pigs can easily solve mazes. They also show an understanding of language that's written in symbols and have excellent memories. They like to play, which is another form of intelligence. They can even learn to push a joystick to make a cursor on a computer screen move!

OCTOPUSES

Octopuses have the largest amount of brainpower of all invertebrate species. Surprisingly, about three-fifths of the 130 million neurons an octopus has are in its eight arms instead of in its head! The arms can be thinking about grabbing something to eat while the brain in its head is solving another problem. Octopuses can learn by watching another octopus doing something in a tank next to theirs.

Common Octopus

ANIMALS ARE AMAZING!

It's difficult to measure the intelligence of animals because they are so different than human beings. However, as scientists continue to study the types of intelligence that animals display, they are gaining a better understanding of human intelligence. Many intelligent animals feel compassion for each other, play fight like brothers do, communicate with one another, form friendships, use tools, and recognize themselves when they look in a mirror.

Awesome! Now that you know more about intelligent animals, you can read more about nocturnal animals in the Baby Professor book Animals That Hunt in the Dark.

Visit
BABY PROFESSOR
EDUCATION KIDS
www.BabyProfessorBooks.com
to download Free Baby Professor eBooks
and view our catalog of new and exciting
Children's Books